Using Grief to Grow: A Primer
~ *How to Help/ How to Get Help*

Johnette Hartnett

Published by Good Mourning, P.O. 9355, South Burlington, VT 05407-9355; distributed by same.

ISBN: 1-883171-96-2 (Volume 1)
ISBN: 1-883171-81-4 (6 Volume Set)
Library of Congress Catalog Card Number: 93-90774

The Good Mourning Series has been partially funded by a grant from the National Funeral Directors Association (NFDA).

This book is dedicated to my three cherubs,
as I so often called them.

DAVID JOHN
July 4, 1971 - March 8, 1983

JOHNETTE THERESE
December 19, 1972 - March 8, 1983

JOHN PETER
May 28, 1974 - March 8, 1983

All your past except its beauty is gone,
and nothing is left but a blessing.
                    – A Course in Miracles

Using Grief to Grow: A Primer
~ How You Can Help/How to Get Help

Contents

Foreword 1

Introduction..7

Stages of Grief 10

Reactions to Grief 33

Society and Grief 55

Families and Grief...71

Footnotes/References 84

Order Form 85

Foreword

On March 8, 1983, my three children and housekeeper died in a fire in St. Albans, Vermont. My son David John was eleven years old; my daughter, Johnette Therese, was nine; and my son John Peter was eight. Our housekeeper, Nancy, was twenty-one.

Until that day I was a busy and happy woman. Although I was facing a divorce, my life was full with children, a busy professional career and rewarding community work.

Until that day, I belonged to an elite and extremely fortunate group of people to whom such tragedies simply did not happen. We lived in an idyllic small New England town, conspicuously and deliberately lacking the traffic, crime and social ills that plague big cities. We watched those things happen to other people in the movies and on TV or in the newspapers. In our insulated, tight-knit community, we were protected. We were financially secure and the children were healthy, intelligent, talented and athletic. Nothing could happen to us.

Then in the spark of a smoldering ember, our defenses failed, the plan to keep us safe from unspeakable horror disintegrated, and the unimaginable became a reality.

Not one, but all three of my children died. Together. Of smoke inhalation.

The effects, I probably do not need to tell you, have been excruciating, deep and lasting. During the first five years following the fire, I spent many, many hours in therapy sorting out the sometimes sordid events that led to and followed the tragedy. My therapy included sessions with three different professionals whose unique perspectives offered valuable guidance and counsel at different stages of my grief.

In addition to seeking professional help, I amassed a personal arsenal to guard against the waves of pain that to this day rise and subside in a sometimes destructive, sometimes therapeutic sea of sadness.

I have aggressively sought out detailed information on grief and the painful aftermath of death. In the past ten years, I have collected a library of research and attended countless seminars, workshops and professional-level courses. I've spent long hours among practitioners in the fields of mental health, grief, funeral and health-care. Through widening ripples of friendships and business associates, I have met, counseled and learned from others who have lost loved ones and who are searching for the same solace I seek.

Freud said that grief is a natural response to loss. I believe that Freud and his modern successors do not go far enough. For many people who have never experienced a loss, this "natural response" certainly seems like anything *but* natural or normal when it happens to you.

Cultural changes that have taken place over the last fifty to one hundred years have made grief all the more unnatural: Strong religious and community ties, close family units, well-preserved ceremonies and traditions used to lend unfailing support to bereaved families and friends. So many of those traditions have fallen by the wayside. As a culture we have handed over the care of our dying, our aged and our dead to institutions. A century ago, eighty percent of Americans died at home; today, eighty percent die in institutions. We are ignoring death until it hits us squarely in the face. Even then, we are trying to pretend it doesn't happen: Many cremations and burials take place without a funeral or memorial service of any kind.

At the same time, funeral directors are reporting a revealing and rather sad trend: Because funeral professionals are the only association many bereaved people have with death, grieving family members are drifting back to funeral homes for grief support, months after the deaths of their loved ones.

Not only do we lack knowledge of what to do, how to act or how to resolve grief issues for ourselves, we are also adrift and uncomfortable when faced with friends and acquaintances who are grieving. Amazingly, while I struggled with my grief, friends slowly dropped out of my life. The overprotective remark I always got when I asked, "Why? Why doesn't So-and-So call?" was, "You must understand, Johnette, people just don't know what to do or say." I would wonder how these people thought *I* would handle losing my whole family. I had never lost a whole family before. I didn't understand how to do it. I often found myself comforting *others* because of my loss. I became the expert on how to survive tragedy. In order to survive I had to teach others about loss.

Finally, like many people valiantly paddling in the wake of tragedy and grief, I have come to believe that perhaps the only way to make sense of the chaos is to help others. While many people are blessed with an innate ability to communicate compassion and strength and perspective in the presence of the bereaved, many more people are not so blessed.

I have seen a dire need to help people identify, understand and prepare for the process of grief.

Using Grief to Grow: A Primer ~ How You Can Help/How to Get Help is the first in a series of six books I have written to address some of the most common issues I've come across in my recovery and in my research.

The entire series includes:

1. *Using Grief to Grow: A Primer*
   How You Can Help/How to Get Help

2. *Different Losses Different Issues:*
   What to Expect and How to Help.

3. *The Funeral: An Endangered Tradition*
   Making Sense of the Final Farewell

4. *Grief in the Workplace:*
   40 Hours Plus Overtime

5. *Children and Grief:*
   Big Issues for Little Hearts

6. *Death Etiquette for the '90s:*
   What to Do/What to Say

These books are written in an easy-to-pick-up, browse and digest, question-and-answer format. I have attempted to be complete without being overwhelming.

Some issues are supplemented with supporting anecdotes, separated from the rest of the text by this symbol: ❧.

In addition, I refer throughout the text to my other books, which may expand on questions of particular interest to you.

Please accept my sincere hope that you and the bereaved person you are concerned about will benefit from these practical, sensible books.

Johnette Hartnett
Burlington, VT 1993

Introduction

We've all experienced the "what to do" for broken bones, childhood illness, psychological problems due to stress, and various other common medical problems that have become part of our everyday lives. As a culture we have become sophisticated "laymen" when dealing with the medical world. We don't generally think of grief as we would a broken arm, a common cold, or anxiety created by a "Type-A" personality. We refer to the old adage "time heals all wounds" when we discuss grief. Unfortunately, if the grief process isn't "set" like a broken bone, it may never mend. Unresolved grief can slowly penetrate many aspects of our lives without our even knowing it. Left untreated, grief will cloud our perceptions about ourselves, others in our lives and our surroundings. In recent studies, long-term unresolved grief is found to contribute to such problems as terminal illnesses, addictions, broken marriages, lost jobs, and mental illnesses.

Over the past ten years, extensive work has been done in the area of thanatology (the study of death). However, much of it is for the professional or bereaved individuals. Little has been written for the "layman" or what I call the "non-bereaved." For the sake of definition, the non-bereaved are the people challenged with the awesome task of simultaneously being a friend, "shrink," religious advisor, housekeeper, accountant, co-worker, companion, and sometime-philosopher to a recently bereaved friend.

The non-bereaved often fall into these tasks without warning or training.

This book focuses mainly on grief related to death losses. However, it is important to note that failed marriages, lost jobs, relocations, divorces, and similar losses produce a grief in ways similar to the grief caused by the death of a loved one. A death is a very obvious loss. Non-death losses are not. Many go unrecognized and untreated. Often it isn't until people have a loss due to a death that they begin to recognize other losses. A loss does not have to be "socially acceptable" in order to cause grief. Although this book on grief is focused on death losses, it could very well apply to non-death losses.

People who are not in touch with their own grief will have a difficult time supporting bereaved friends. The "catch-22" for the non-bereaved is realizing that everyone is bereaved in some way, even though none of their loved ones have died. Helping friends deal with their losses forces people to look at their own losses – sometimes for the first time.

Questions in this book were chosen from those I hear most often from people who are trying to support bereaved friends. They are also questions that I frequently asked as a mother grieving the death of my children.

The format is question/answer/anecdote. I rely heavily, throughout the book, on my personal experiences to illustrate many of the questions. You will see the irony and contradictions that often show up between the "how to" answer and my own story. It confirms the theory that each grief is uniquely experienced and that sometimes there simply is no "right" way to grieve.

One editor who reviewed this book in its early stages said that "many of the 'how to' answers seem to contain too little 'hard' information." In a way that is correct. Few "hard" facts surface when dealing with grief. I write about the most common symptoms and stages based on the most current research on grief. But even these characteristics vary tremendously from individual to individual. What is important in dealing with the grief process, either from a bereaved or non-bereaved point of view, is identifying feelings, allowing yourself to feel them, and releasing them when you are ready.

It is my wish that this book on grief will help trigger in you an awareness of your individual feelings as they relate to listening, understanding, and communicating with the bereaved. It is through this awareness that the "hard" information about grief becomes exposed, not in the written word.

Stages of Grief

What are the stages/dimensions of grief?

There is a lot of controversy today in some academic circles of grief educators about which "grief model" is best or most accepted. Although I am familiar with several models, I have chosen to use the classic model developed by Dr. Elisabeth Kübler-Ross.[1] In a non-traditional way, I adopted her model for dealing with terminal illness as I worked through my own loss (of sudden death). At that time, there were no other popular models, so I adapted hers to help me work through my loss.

The danger of using a model "with stages," as this one does, is that grief doesn't always follow set stages. Some grief doesn't even go through all stages. However, there are definite parameters in grieving, and being *aware* of those parameters is important. It is best that we *don't* even try to *guess* what stage our bereaved friend might be in.

Remember that when we grieve, we will B-SAAD. These letters represent the five stages of grief listed here. B-SAAD will be our code so we will not forget what the stages are. I also think of the stages of grief as five balloons that overlap and share the same oxygen. A bereaved person can move in and out of a stage, from one balloon to the other, then back again.

Important Note: The stages of grief *almost never* follow any set order. B-SAAD is an anagram I devised to help remember the stages, which occur in different sequences for each individual. Some individuals might never experience all the stages mentioned here.

Bargaining-SAAD

We've all been in this stage at one time or another. Not unlike a child, we make promises to ourselves, our God, and whomever else will listen, to do whatever it takes so the terrible nightmare will disappear. We will give up virtually anything to alter the course that has changed our lives so tragically. If all it took to cure the world of terminal illness and tragedy was personal will power, it would have happened long ago. "Just one more chance" is the fantasy we all experience in this stage of grief.

ॐ

My brother was dying of cancer of the eye when I was fourteen and he was ten. I used to promise God every night that I would give up whatever He wanted if He would make my brother well. It didn't work. My brother died anyway.

I used to wake up in the mornings after the children died and – for just a few minutes – feel "normal." Then, all of the sudden the whole horror would rush back into my head. In disbelief, I'd realize they were gone. I will never see them again. I could do nothing to change the fact that they were dead. There wasn't any deal to make. I knew that.

B-*Shock* AAD

A father who finds out that his daughter just died or a woman who discovers that her husband has terminal cancer, or that a best friend has AIDS, is likely to go numb.

If we can visualize this same person inside a huge block of ice, then we have a good picture of what the shock stage of grief is all about. Our bodies protect us when we get an overdose of bad news. How long we stay in this block of ice depends on the manner of death our loved one has experienced and the type of coping (or thawing) skills we have.

People in the state of shock might appear to be functioning quite well and have a high energy level. This "disguise" is the body's way of protecting itself. As we begin to "melt" we start to move out of this stage. The shock stage can last weeks, months, or in extreme cases, years.

As I was driving home the morning of the fire I heard the news on the radio. As I turned into the street I saw the trucks. Everything was gone. My ex-husband was there. Stunned. Friends. Neighbors. I went to my parents' house next door.

It was like a slow-motion movie. I asked my ex-husband to stay with me. I looked around and he was gone. My mother rolled up her Oriental rug as people came through the front door. My mother told me to go to bed and rest. I didn't want to be alone. I wanted to go into the burned house. Everyone said no. My father went with me. I found the remains of photo albums. That was all that was left. There was indeed a fire. The popcorn bowl was still on the family room floor. Empty. My last gesture as a mother. I made them popcorn before I left that night.

I went into their bedrooms. My son's portable radio had melted to the night stand. Their beds were empty. They were gone. They died of smoke inhalation I was told. It was a thousand degrees in the house during the fire. I looked at their bedroom windows, the red decals were there. They had brought them home during National Fire Prevention week in October. What a joke. The decals made it, but the children didn't. I turned to my father and told him we could leave. I'd seen all I needed to see.

Shortly after the fire I moved to Chicago. I was probably in shock for the two years I lived there. People I worked with closely knew about the fire; others never knew. I just went on from day to day. I was dealing with my grief "externally." That's how I coped.

It wasn't until I returned to Vermont that the ice block started to melt and my grief work moved into a new dimension.

B-S*Anger* AD

When someone we love is dying or has just died, we get angry. Often we express this anger in blame. Usually we blame the doctors, the hospital, society, friends, relatives, work, the funeral director, circumstances, ourselves, or the deceased.

If we are religious, we might even blame God for allowing *this* to happen.

But most often we blame ourselves. When we turn anger inward we get depressed. So here we find ourselves in the depression stage of the grief cycle. (A certain degree of depression is normal during the grief process; for some, this can become full-blown clinical depression.) Most of us have to do all the blaming first before we can begin to even look at ourselves. Admitting that WE FEEL guilty and responsible for another's death is scary. Understanding WHY we feel this way takes time and hard work. If this stage of grief gets "put on hold" indefinitely (which it often does), it can permanently distort our self-esteem.

So if your recently bereaved friend seems mighty angry at the world, he is. He might even lash out at you for no apparent reason. Try to understand that his lashing out, although misdirected, is normal.

You might have told your bereaved friend fifty times the logical facts surrounding his loss, and for some reason it doesn't sink in; you wonder if he is ever going to get it. He will. It takes time and patience. Bear with him. He needs to explore each minute detail himself.

The anger stage of grief is sort of the "net-net bottom line" of friendship for the

If Your Friend Seems Angry at the World, He Probably Is

bereaved. Many friendships drift apart during this difficult time. Grief has a way of turning friendships into gold or rust.

Expressing anger has always been difficult for me. I probably was most angry at myself for not being home the night of the fire. It took a lot of work to acknowledge the fact that if I had been there I probably would have died also. A part of me doesn't believe that, but I have learned to at least acknowledge it. The guilt of feeling responsible for the deaths of four people is not easily dismissed.

Not knowing what happened the night of the fire, how much the children and their housekeeper suffered, are unanswerable questions. They are the black box that will never be opened. I've learned to accept that intellectually. I still have difficulty with it in my heart.

I've gone through periods in which I was angry at the children for leaving me. How did they expect me to go on without them? Why didn't they escape? Unanswerable questions I know, but nevertheless very real to me for a long time. I was angry at the fire department. I had decals on the children's bedroom windows. They never put the hook and ladder up to their second story windows. Why couldn't they have saved my children?

I've been angry at my ex-husband for not being what I wanted him to be. I have often thought if we had not gotten divorced, maybe the fire would not have happened.

I've been angry at people for not knowing what to do or say. So many times my friends would tell me to try and understand. People just are at a loss as to what to do or say. "What about me?" I would always say. This was new to me, too. I'd never lost three children before. Angry. I was very angry. And scared.

I think about my anger; it has been directed mostly at myself. The feeling that there had to be something I could have done to save my children's lives is always nearby.

The anger dimension of my grief process has diminished. But surprisingly, when least expected, it is triggered by some issues that I have not completely or satisfactorily dealt with.

One positive way I vented my anger was through a law suit over the cause of the fire. It was a long and involved case and gave me the opportunity to sift through records and information pertaining to the fire. Listening to the experts, hearing the facts, helped me to accept (although not completely) that we had not been careless and reckless. It just so happened that a series of mistakes caused four deaths.

The trial was a turning point for me. I now needed to look ahead to what I wanted to do the rest of my life. The trial helped me put away the business of the fire. It was a release. Packing up the files after the lawsuit was a good-bye to that part of my life. It was scary. What was my cause now?

B-SA*Acceptance* D

Accepting the reality of a loss in one's life is indeed hard. Although the stages of grief do not happen in order, this stage, acceptance, is usually the final stage of grief. Remembering the balloon analogy, one might drift in and out of acceptance for quite a long time. It is accepting and letting go of our past and moving into our future that marks this stage of grief.

If your bereaved friend starts talking about the future, working out again (yes, on her own without begging from you), volunteering, buying new clothes (basically stops wearing the grief colors), wants to go dancing, suggests changing a tradition, becomes concerned about her diet, etc., then she's probably moving into acceptance. When the grieving person finally internalizes the reality of her loss, a sense of purpose comes into focus. For those of you who have been close to your friend throughout her grief process, it will be quite obvious.

But a word of warning. Acceptance doesn't mean forgetting. Your bereaved friend will never forget her loss. There will be setbacks. There still will be the "what ifs" and the "poor me(s)," especially during holidays, anniversaries and birthdays.[2]

One Can Drift In and Out of the Stages of Grief for Quite a Long Time

Acceptance represents a release from the past. At first your bereaved friend might feel strange or guilty with her new-found "freedom." You might, too. In a way you have both been preoccupied for a long time with the business of grieving. Getting on with life and finding new meaning is now the challenge for the person who finally accepts her loss.

ॐ

As I write this book, I get glimpses of how much I've lost. I don't look at the whole, big picture very often. I've learned to compartmentalize my loss. In that way I deal with pieces of it at a time.

Over the holidays one year I met a couple who had buried their grown up son five years before. He had committed suicide. The couple had two adult daughters, grandchildren, and sons-in-law. We spoke at length about their children and their lives. They spoke little about their dead son. When they did, very fresh grief entered their voices and their eyes. As I returned home that night I wondered why I didn't have at least one of my children left. Not that I would have chosen which one to survive. The magnitude of my loss seemed overwhelming that night. I shared it with a friend. We cried together. We agreed none of it is fair.

And yet I know I have accepted my loss. What I'm seeing is that I will slip in and out of acceptance. From one balloon to another. My life is focused and meaningful. It took me almost five years after the children died to begin to feel good again. Even happy at times.

Accepting my loss without bitterness will be my life challenge. As I vacillate from one balloon to the other and back, I continually re-position myself and my loss so it works for me today. Tomorrow is another day.

B-SAA*Denial*

Denial is a temporary band-aid we've all used to avoid reality. When a situation, whether a terminal illness, non-death loss, or death loss occurs, we often use denial to cope. That's not all bad. Denial that's used to help cushion the blow of a loss is normal and healthy. However, denial used to ignore the pain of a loss may permanently "put on hold" the normal grief process.

We all know denial in our lives. We sometimes call it procrastination, but it isn't. Procrastinators usually know they are procrastinating. Often, people don't know they are in denial. It makes sense when you think about it. The trick in denial is precisely that. You pretend something doesn't exist.

When the reality of death hits a person, he either deals with it or makes substitutes. In order to substitute the reality of a death, a person uses denial. It's the perfect answer to combating reality.

So if your bereaved friend seems to be avoiding the reality of his loss, understand that he is going through a normal dimension in the grief process.

Some People Get "Stuck" in Denial

Some people get stuck in this stage of grief. We've all met those people. Twenty years after their loss they are still blaming and projecting their guilt onto the world. If you see this occurring in your friend, gently suggest therapy. Don't judge. Coming to terms with a tragic loss is most difficult. Resolving denial is critical to getting on with one's life.

ʘ

I avoided writing about this stage of grief for a long time. I just could not think of where my denial has been in my grief process. The reason I didn't see the denial was that I was looking in the all-too-obvious places. I was looking for a denial that would have hindered me from accepting my loss. But instead I found a denial that helped me substitute my loss. It was very clever indeed. I found my denial in a very strange but not unusual place – in my personal relationship.

At the time of the fire I was involved with a married man. We were the classic example. I was getting divorced, he was going to do the same soon after. He knew the children. When the fire happened, life became very serious for both of us. I needed support and love. He gave me what he could. He listened to me for endless hours. Long distance. Wherever I was in the country, we talked daily. But he didn't leave his wife.

Eventually I came to understand that he had been, among other things, my last link to the children and a life that I shared with them. Letting go of him was not an option for a long, long time.

I had been unable to look at the limits in my relationship. They are outdated and reflect a very different woman from the one I have become. However, it has been through my grief that the issue of my relationships with men is emerging. The child in me has always tried to please. The woman in me has never known real intimacy or self esteem. I've always been attracted to men I've wanted to change.

I faced most of my grief head-on. I became comfortable with the denial in my personal life. I would rationalize that I just couldn't handle another loss. That my personal life had nothing to do with my loss. I really could not imagine another change. The man in my life told me things would change, soon. I believed him. Just give him a little more time. I did. Things weren't that bad. But they were. At a time in my life when I needed support and companionship, I was short-changing myself. I was defending my right to be loved. I was searching for a solution for someone else's life. I was putting _me_ on hold. I was building my self-esteem in one area of my life and tearing it down in another.

I'd been pretending that everything would get better if I worked hard at getting my mental and physical health back on line. I had separated my grief from my personal life without realizing that they are very much intertwined. What I did not see was that my grief is a composite of all my losses. It affects very much how I feel about myself and how I relate to others in my life.

What steps can the bereaved take to complete their grief work?[3]

1. Emotionally detach themselves from the deceased

The type of loss will dictate the emotional involvement the bereaved has with the deceased. A mother, for instance, will find it quite difficult to stop thinking in terms of her child's safety and well-being. She might repeat certain behaviors every day until the reality of her child's absence and death sets in. She will need to begin to focus her emotional energy on the living. This by no means suggests that she will forget her child. The process of detaching herself emotionally from her dead child and channeling new energies into other relationships is a difficult but necessary process in resolving grief.

... From Wife to Widow, from Brother to Only Child

2. Adjust to a world without their loved one

Mothers, fathers, sisters, brothers, aunts, cousins, husbands, wives all need to make major adjustments when they lose a loved one. A death can be like a demotion in the pecking order of life. From a wife to a widow, a husband to a widower, a mother to an ex-mother, a sister/brother to an only child and on and on. New identities. The bereaved have to adjust financially, emotionally, physically, and socially to the consequences of their loss.

3. Build New Relationships

Getting on with life is definitely the challenge for the bereaved in this final task of re-entering life. Risking and investing in new relationships is a sign that the bereaved are completing their grief work.

Cooking and mealtime were always an integral part of my family life. Cutting my menu down from five people to one was difficult. Mastering simple specialties, participating in neighborhood cookie exchanges. I always loved dinner with the children, and emotionally, I still have a hard time at supper time. I seldom eat at home alone. I usually work through the supper hour. I often plan my main meal at noon, or plan to meet a friend for an evening meal together. It wasn't until five years after the children died that I began to invite friends in and to cook again. I started a garden and found great pleasure in growing vegetables and flowers.

What is anticipatory grief?[4]

Anticipatory grief usually refers to a process families or friends go through when dealing with the terminally ill. This grief is similar to the grief experienced after the death of a loved one, except that it begins before the actual death.

Anticipatory grief can be therapeutic in helping the bereaved make the transition when their loved one dies. However, studies indicate that too much anticipatory grief can produce a premature detachment from the dying patient. If the expected loss does not occur, such as the return of a POW or a remission in a cancer patient, the detachment may be difficult to reverse. A good example is the high rate of divorce among returning POWs after the Viet Nam War. Many families were unable to re-invest an emotional attachment to their loved one. It is important for the non-bereaved to note that anticipatory grief does not pave the way for a "grief-free" recovery for the bereaved.

It was June and my sister, my father and I had all just celebrated a combined graduation party – me from eighth grade, my sister from high school, and my dad had earned a Ph.D. in biochemistry. The day after our party I was standing in the hall of our home when the lab called from the hospital with news of my brother's biopsy on his eye tissue. Malignant. My father sat down and wept. I stood there knowing that it was going to be all right. It had to be.

That day, almost two years before my brother died, was the beginning of our grief as a family. The long road of my brother's terminal illness was ahead of us; none of us fully comprehended what that meant. None of us understood the business of grieving that would change our family dynamics.

Because of the nature of my brother's cancer, his suffering surpassed the limits of hope for healing or remission. Toward the end, we welcomed his death as the only option for relieving him of his pain.

Of course I can write that because I was not his mother. I cannot imagine the pain my mother must have felt knowing that death was, in the end, the only painkiller for her only son.

When my children died, there was absolutely no forewarning or anticipation of the impending tragedy. There was no time to sort out what I would do or how I would feel. It was horror.

Should people see a medical doctor or grief therapist while grieving?

How to deal with the overwhelming pain of a deep personal loss is tricky business that often requires help from trained professionals.

Probably the last thing most people who have suffered a loss want to do is sit down with a stranger and talk about their loved one. A visit to a family physician is a good idea. Because of the insidious nature of grief, it is only good preventive mental health to consider a therapist, especially if the death was sudden or involved a child.

It is not unusual for a recently bereaved person to have feelings of depression, anger, fatigue, disorganization, denial, sadness, and suicide.

Bereaved people are susceptible to numerous illnesses – physical as well as psychological. Checking in with a family physician or therapist after a loss makes good sense. The old days of "we'll get through this ourselves" are really gone.

During the two years following the fire, my therapist in Chicago became very much my confidant and friend. My aunt and I used to refer to him as the "wizard." It seemed he always put things in perspective. When I thought I was truly crazy he always made everything seem so normal.

With my move back to Vermont two years later, I thought the need for therapy was over. Little did I realize that I was moving into a new dimension of my grief process. My Vermont therapist pulled no punches. He told me flat out about the long haul I had ahead of me. I will never forget that time. I felt like everything had been pulled out from under me.

For me, counseling has been a major factor in my recovery. Without the constant questioning and re-positioning I've done, I never would be where I am today. I was forced to make changes and to look at *me*. Whether I would have chosen this route independent of my tragedy I'm not sure. It hasn't been easy.

The single most important benefit of my counseling, initially, was learning about grief. Being reassured that the feelings and reactions I was having were normal and very much part of the "grief work" helped me. Therapy kept me in touch with my inner feelings on a regular basis. Something that was new to me.

Subsequent therapy wasn't so much over my children's death, but more focused on the issues of finding out who I am. Their deaths began the process of peeling away layer after layer in search of the person within me. Although this process will probably never be over, it has helped me grow into a more compassionate, accepting woman, instead of a bitter, angry ex-wife and ex-mother.

Although I had many losses before in my life, I'd never learned anything about grief. In those days no one acknowledged my losses. I remember missing my maternal grandmother so much. And my brother. But there was no one to share these feelings with. Life just went on. If we didn't talk about our losses, the unspoken rule seemed to be, they would go away. But of course they didn't.

Is it correct to use the word "recover" when talking about "getting on with one's life" after a loss?

The word "recovery" is tricky because it suggests being well again. Being the "recoveree" requires dealing with all the new feelings of getting on with life. Being recovered from grief is different than recovering from a cold or flu. After a cold things are pretty much the same for a person as they were before. Not so with grief. After a loss, most people's priorities and outlooks go through some changes, sometimes minor, often major. It is safe to say that if your bereaved friend is adjusting to her loss with a positive and productive attitude, then the process of recovery has started.

Recovery requires fine-tuning our losses so we can integrate them into our present and future lives. Some say recovery is a lifelong process.

Recovery Requires Us to Fine-tune Our Losses

As one good friend said to me, "I would assess your recovery from this personal holocaust at ninety-five percent. Even you would admit to sixty percent."

My friend is probably not too far off from my personal assessment. There has been a recovery in my life. The overall grief that has been added to my life will never go away, it shadows every decision I make. It is my choice to use this added dimension to better myself or to live in the past.

People often say I look good considering what I've been through. I usually feel guilty after, thinking maybe I shouldn't dress up or wear make-up. Or maybe I'm not grieving right. Or people will tell me they could have never gone through what I did. Then I usually feel like a freak. I sometimes wonder myself, how did I go through it? Why did I survive?

But I feel renewed and clear. I like myself. Maybe this is recovery.

How long does grief last?

When asked, "How long does grief last?" one therapist responded, "How far is up?"

One research study interviewed people on the street asking them how long they thought grief lasted. The average answer was two weeks. The experts say around three years (especially when the loss is a child), though most professionals are very reluctant to give time lines.

Trying to pinpoint timeframes for grief is futile. We tend to want to hurry up this process because of all of the uncomfortable implications about life, death, pain, and sorrow. We think if we know how long grief is going to last it will make it easier somehow.

As a non-bereaved bystander, being _aware_ of the timeframe surrounding grief will help you in planning your commitment to your friend.

ða

My decision to return home and deal with my grief "first hand" was not a popular decision among my family members, and close friends. Many thought I should just stay away and get on with my life. For me, coming home to Vermont and working through the rest of my grief was essential for my "getting better." I had to make that decision. Your bereaved friends will have to make similar difficult decisions. Try to support them in their process even if you would do it differently.

The summer of 1987 marked a definite shift in my grief. It was literally like someone had lifted something off me. I

would remark to friends that I would wake
up in the morning and peek out from
under the covers wondering if IT was still
gone. A little dramatic sounding, but very
much the way I felt. There was a renewed
sense of purpose and more energy than I
had had in the four and one-half years
since the kids had died.

Reactions to Grief

Why is it normal for bereaved adults and children to be repetitious about their loss?

Freud called it "obsessional review," this
need we have to go over and over
information until it becomes a reality for
us.

A young child will listen to a story about
his grandmother's death and seem to
understand, ask questions, and listen
attentively. It isn't unusual for that same
child to wake up the next morning and
ask when he can see his grandmother
again. The child is dealing with his grief
according to his maturity and
understanding.[5]

Does your bereaved friend go over and
over facts surrounding his loss that you've
heard at least a hundred times? Understand
that this process is critical to your friend's
grief work. Listen. You make a difference

for your friend. Just being present allows him to sift through this information. He needs to do it.

Picture the wheel of fortune going round and round, stopping, going, stopping. That is what is happening inside of your friend's mind. He is trying out the same story, over and over again, sometimes with a little different twist, to see what will work. What he can digest. What he can throw out. What he can accept. What he can learn to live with.

For me the lawsuit over the house fire gave me a forum for reviewing the facts surrounding the fire _ad nauseum_. I spent about two years very absorbed in the business of the fire. When the trial was finally over and my files packed away, I still didn't have my children back. Sometimes I thought if I worked hard enough the children would return.

What physical symptoms accompany grief?

Grief can cause panic attacks, irritability, inability to sleep, ulcers, weight loss or gain, crying, physical and mental exhaustion, memory loss, tooth decay, ingrown toe nails, psoriasis, emotional illness, etc. Although the above symptoms may seem slightly exaggerated, grief does cause tremendous stress physiologically and psychologically. How much this stress affects an individual depends on an infinite number of genetic, environmental, and psychological variables that are unique to each human being.

The other pain, the broken heart pain, is not so easy to predict or discuss. The remedy or prescription for the broken heart requires self-love and understanding. Learning to live fully without your mate, child, parent, friend, lover, takes an enormous amount of work and energy. To a non-bereaved friend, this pain is probably most difficult to understand because of the sensitive mortality issue it seems to stir up. When we confront our friend's pain of loss, we'll confront our own.

The Remedy for a Broken Heart Requires Self-love and Understanding

&

I experienced panic attacks frequently. On and off for two years. At first I felt like I was having a heart attack. I soon realized that the tightness in my throat or chest (which lasted several minutes or so) was related to my grief. Many bereaved people I have talked with experience these attacks; others do not.

The pain of the broken heart has been the most chronic pain for me. It pops up in funny places. Seeing a Red Skins jacket (my two sons used to wear them), the passing of another birthday, going through the holidays, seeing one of their friends who is now six feet tall, brings back that old familiar pang. The broken heart pain does not devastate me the way it used to. I think the secret is to accept the pain, feel it, and let it go.

As I have come to terms with this pain, I know I would never want to lose the memory of my children in order to be "grief-free." Maybe this is the "sweet sorrow" that the poets have written about for centuries.

Is grief a sign of emotional weakness?

Everyone experiences grief after a loss regardless of their emotional and psychological make up. Some people are more vulnerable to a loss than others. This vulnerability is unique to each individual.

We remark when someone has been "strong" or "dignified" throughout a tragedy. We admire strength. We admire poise. We dislike weakness and emotional outbursts. Many of us are uncomfortable seeing a man cry. We often equate toughness with strength, with coping, with "okayness." We often judge how people are doing by their external behavior. Many bereaved give off "okay" vibes when, in fact, they are empty inside.

It is important for you to be aware that the external behavior you observe in your bereaved friend is not necessarily what is going on inside of him. Try to become sensitive to the many masks of grief.

A good friend of mine told me how lucky I was to have good mental health. I had never thought about having "good mental health"; I'd always taken that for granted. There have been many times throughout my grief process when I just didn't think I could make it through one more hour or one more day. But I did. I think of my friend's words often, especially when I find coping more difficult than usual. I've grown to accept that there will be difficult times and road blocks. My grief work has had a clever way of turning many of my weaknesses into strengths.

Does working and keeping busy help cure grief?

If the only prescription for fixing grief was hard work, grief would be extinct. Keeping busy has become the general prescription for dealing with losses. We think somehow, by working harder, grief will just go away. Time does not heal all wounds. And neither does work. For many, keeping busy seems like the only option to getting through a loss. It isn't.

Using denial to cope with loss is good if it is used to lighten the initial blow of the loss. So working harder right after a loss isn't always the wrong thing to do. When your bereaved friend becomes obsessed with work and overcome with fatigue but won't give up, be aware. Don't shrug off his behavior with, "He's been under a lot of stress lately." Suggest a visit to his family physician or an appointment with a grief therapist. Offer to go with him.

Grief is like a Full-time Job with No Pay.

Grieving is like having another job. You just don't get paid for it. For most bereaved, life has to go on. They work, they pay bills, they take care of families and ... they grieve.

Dealing with grief "externally" is okay for awhile. If you are an employer, your bereaved employee might seem extremely efficient and productive initially. Beware. At some point your employee may begin to internalize his loss. It is at this point that the "grief work" combined with regular work will become a challenge for him.[6]

❧

Immediately after the fire that took the lives of my children, I flew to Chicago to be with my Midwest family. Very early one morning I found myself up and dressed and asking my uncle to take me to work with him. I worked for the next two years. I really thought if I worked hard enough the pain inside would go away. The work made me tired and helped me forget my loss for a few hours at a time.

When I returned to Vermont two years later I realized (much to my horror) that I had only begun my grief work. The emotional stress of my loss had taken its toll. I was mentally and physically exhausted. Friends constantly comforted me in my "temporary" situation. I spent hours comparing my life to the lives of others, trying to find a formula that would instantly transform my life so it would be like the lives of my friends. (I really believed that, too.) I wanted to be involved in life again. I felt like I was on the outside looking in. I was. I just wanted someone to tell me what to do with my life. I felt incapable of making decisions.

I started to realize that my own "work ethic" had been centered around parental approval. Long before the children died I had worked and volunteered to get validation for the person that was me. In my grief, that formula didn't work anymore. The harder I worked or the less I worked didn't solve the issues I needed to deal with. I didn't seem to have a balance.

I had learned to define who I was by the work I did. If I wasn't performing and successful then I did not feel worthwhile.

Although my work now is very much a part of my life, it is not my life. I have found meaning and a sense of purpose from my work. But if I lost it all tomorrow (as I did when my office burned with the house) I would survive. I know I could start over, build again and find new meaning.

What about alcohol and drugs during grief?

Sedating grief feelings only prolongs the business of grieving. In many cases what was only intended as a quick fix for the immediate pain of a tragedy can develop into or trigger a long-term drug or alcohol dependency.

A Quick Fix for Immediate Pain May Trigger a Long-term Drug or Alcohol Dependency

There probably isn't a person in the world who is likely to deny a friend a drink after burying a loved one. It all seems so harmless. But much of the grief process can be aborted or distorted by abusing alcohol or drugs on a daily basis.

Being aware of the potential dangerous effects that alcohol or drugs can have on a recently bereaved friend's grief process helps you to effectively support your friend. Encourage your bereaved friend in recreational outlets that don't include drinking. Whether your friend is susceptible to a potential alcohol/drug problem is not the issue. You'd never invite bereaved friends out for a social drinking evening and say, "Well, let's go out and get depressed. After all you've been through what's another depressant?"

After the children died my social drinking picked up. I had always been a more than average social drinker (of course I never thought I was). I had developed quite a tolerance. No one said anything to me for the first few years. How could they? We were *all* groping for ways to survive. I was sedating my feelings of pain more and more often with alcohol. I was defeating much of the benefit of therapy.

I started using alcohol as a painkiller. I fooled myself into thinking that I was drug-free. I never took Valium or any anti-depressants.

Time passed. Friends started mentioning to me that I should cut back. I started to become aware of certain habits. There was rarely a day I didn't drink.

Three and a half years after the children's death I was picked up for Driving While Intoxicated in Vermont. The officer said he stopped me because I had swerved. I was going around thirty-five miles per hour. My Blood Alcohol Level test was 0.19. The law in Vermont for legal drunkenness was 0.1. I could have killed someone. I could have killed myself.

I was ashamed and scared. I had a problem. I knew that. Now it was public. My challenge was to do something about it. I attended the Cork Project at Dartmouth Hitchcock Hospital for an intense forty-eight-hour workshop on alcohol. As I sat through eighteen hours of lectures, films, and group discussions on alcohol, I slowly started to realize that I had to quit drinking. I did in March 1987.

I've learned that alcohol doesn't affect everyone the same way. I had a pre-disposition and a history of social drinking. My tragedy triggered a potential addiction problem that was already in place. My present problems were caused (in large part) from the alcohol, and not just the grief. The more I drank, the less I needed to deal with the pain of my losses. As a recovering alcoholic said to me, "When you drink, things become "shrugoffable."

I know I could have used the drinking as an excuse for not getting on with my life. And probably, with what I had been through, I could have justified it. It took a policeman to wake me up to what I was doing to myself and the potential tragedy I could have brought to others. I thank God for that policeman.

Does feeling uncomfortable and embarrassed about grief affect how people cope with grief?

When we don't know much about a subject we often feel uncomfortable dealing with it. Death certainly falls into this category,

Many people judge how someone is feeling by his external appearance and behavior. How many times have you heard someone admire behavior at a funeral because it appears to be "strong" or "brave?" We seldom verbally admire someone who breaks down at a wake or funeral. We say they're "taking it real hard" or, "they've always been an emotional family." We have done a good job at stereotyping the bereaved.

We still admire a "macho" image about grief. An adult male whose dad had died cried openly at the wake. His mother went around asking his brothers what was wrong with him. Showing any outward signs of emotions is often considered a character flaw or personality weakness. As you begin to understand grief, you will begin to accept outward displays of emotion as normal, not embarrassing or

The "Macho" Male Image and Grief

43

weak, as critical steps in getting better.

Elisabeth Kübler-Ross, a physician who pioneered research about death and dying, has a rule in her Life, Death Transition Seminars: You cannot touch another person. Not even a gentle tap or hug or a pat on the back. For five days. And she means it. I went to one of these seminars and at first I didn't understand. But after a few short hours of the workshop, it became clear that even an innocent touch might interrupt someone from processing their feelings as they relate to what is happening around them. How often when we were young did our mothers touch us and say, "Oh stop crying, everything will be okay." And sometimes we stopped crying, but not because we had worked through anything, but more because we were afraid of what might happen if we did not. Elisabeth's theory makes sense.

Hugging and touching are important, but be sensitive to your friend when he starts to show his emotions. Don't rush over and squelch everything because _you_ want it to be okay. Try to sit back and listen, and maybe when it's all over give a gentle hug.

Elisabeth Kübler-Ross also has encouraged emergency rooms of many hospitals to provide "screaming rooms" for the families of tragic, sudden deaths. They are often staffed by the Compassionate

Friends, a group of parents that get together to grieve the loss of their children. It is Elisabeth's hope that these "screaming rooms" will begin the process of getting the grief out for the survivors. This concept contrasts with the notion of giving tranquilizers to shut down the feelings of the bereaved and sending them home to deal with their grief – alone.

Encourage your bereaved friend to do whatever will make him feel better. Don't be embarrassed to shed your own tears. Letting your friend know that you are feeling his loss is powerful medicine. When we share our friend's loss we share our own. Together, our grief becomes love.

Embarrassment and discomfort about death are not temporary feelings. They are often part of long-held traditions that have never been dealt with. And they often block the bereaved from getting on with their grief. Getting beyond uncomfortable and embarrassing feelings is critical in doing good, effective grief work.

I don't remember crying when my brother died. My sisters repeated the word "supercalofragilisticexbialadosus" to ourselves at the wake so we wouldn't cry. There was a large gathering at my parents' home after the funeral. I remember walking down the main street with my two sisters. We were all dressed in black. We didn't talk about John's death. It was like we all just held our breath wondering if we dared breathe again.

When I was hospitalized a few months after the children's funeral, a psychiatrist who had been a resident during my brother's illness some twenty years before came to see me. She shared with me a rather strange story. She knew my brother and the history of his illness. Our family had been in and out of the hospital over a two-year period while my brother was dying. She told me that the staff at the hospital had used our family as a model family in dealing with a terminally ill family member. The staff offered professional support to our family. My parents said no. We were fine. My brother died and the family sort of just split up. My sister married; I went to camp; my parents went on vacation, alone. We never really talked about John's death. It splintered our lives. We really didn't know what to say or do for each other.

I was amazed to hear this story some twenty years later. When my brother died, we looked like the strong, together family unit. We had masked our grief from each other and the rest of the world.

One of the few demonstrations of grief that I remember is standing next to my father at the grave site when they lowered my brother's casket into the ground. My father sobbed uncontrollably. In his own sorrow he let it be okay for me to grieve with my own tears. Some twenty years later I realized what a gift he'd given me.

Will a geographical change (such as moving) cure grief?

Grief responds first to inner, not outward, change and growth. The advice you always hear when someone has just survived a major loss is to do *nothing* for at least a year. The reason for that is quite obvious. The bereaved need time to process their loss.

For some, a change of scenery is important and even necessary. However the change of scenery does not mean there will be a change of heart. Grief work must be ongoing and progressing in order to benefit from a geographical change. Waiting awhile until the grief work has had time to give back some clarity and focus makes good common sense.

Geographic change doesn't always mean relocating to another state or city. Sometimes the bereaved find it necessary to change their place of residence or work because of reminders they find too painful. This is often the case in suicides or murders that happened in the home.[7]

ॐ

Two weeks after the fire I found myself with family in Chicago. I decided to stay there, and I worked for the next two years. After six months I moved into an apartment in downtown Chicago. It was the first time I'd lived alone in my thirty-three years.

When I was contemplating moving back to Vermont, my psychiatrist in Chicago pointed out that I had only one thing to lose – the cost of the move. If it didn't work out I could always move back to Chicago. With that in mind I reluctantly moved home. The wisdom in his advice was not so evident in those days.

When I returned to Vermont I began to move into a new dimension of my grief. I was shocked. I had really thought I had done all my grief work in Chicago. Being back in Vermont reopened my wounds. At first it was overwhelming.

The next three years proved to be difficult and painful. They represented much growth and change. I know now that had I never gone back to Vermont I would have been unable to complete my grief work. Being back in familiar – though painful – territory helped me deal with the past, accept it, and let it go.

Why do so many people feel so guilty when a friend or family member dies?

We have all gone through the "if only" litany. Feeling responsible for a person's death is a natural response to loss.

I read once that guilt is like currency. We use it over and over again to "pay" for what we think we did wrong. If we feel guilty, we feel like we have paid our dues. And so we repeat the same pattern again and again. With grief, this repetitious behavior causes interference with the normal process of grieving. Falling into the "my-fault quicksand" is a sure way to get sucked up into denial and stay there.

The problem with guilt is that it disguises itself. Often we don't recognize that it is our guilt, and not us, that chooses to remember only selected facts about a death and the deceased.

Guilt is an expert at projecting blame and hatred on its victims. And in return its victims project blame and hatred. Guilt is the "hot potato" of grief. The bereaved keep passing the "hot potato" around. We don't need to experience a death loss to know guilt. But guilt that is born from a death loss is on the graduate school level.

Both bereaved and non-bereaved individuals need to learn that recognizing the origin of guilt is the first step in

Grief and Guilt

49

dealing with it. Doing something about it is second. Learning to deal with the "little guilts" of every day life is a wonderful preparation for combating the "big guilts" that accompany any major loss.

When my brother died I felt guilty. I remembered two incidents: One was about the sleep-over with my girlfriends in our tent in the back yard. My brother, four years younger than I, wanted to sleep with us. I said no. He cried himself to sleep that night. When he died, I thought for sure it had something to do with my selfishness.

The other memory is about his music. I took piano lessons and practiced everyday. He started taking drum lessons and wanted to practice everyday. We argued frequently over who would practice and when. I was older and usually won out. Again I felt his death was due to my selfishness.

I have two sisters, but I was closest in age to my brother. I often wondered why I didn't die. My mother only had one son, but she had three daughters. I think for a long time I felt guilty that he got sick instead of me. I wonder if my proficiency at the piano had anything to do with wanting to make my mother feel better. I can remember after my brother's death playing the piano for hours and hours. I

felt like my music brought my parents
some happiness.

The weekend before my children died,
my daughter wanted majorette boots. They
would have cost $45. I had told her no.
(Knowing that most of the young
majorettes wore chaps over their sneakers,
I told her I would talk to her teacher and
see what all the other children were going
to wear.) She got upset with me and was
somewhat unpleasant the rest of the day. I
often wonder in my weaker moments why
I didn't buy her the darned boots.

My own guilt about my children's death
is much harder to write about. I wasn't
home the night of the fire. I wasn't there
for my children. Someone heard my
daughter crying out for me before she
died. It was the first time I had ever left
them with a paid housekeeper overnight.

I have asked for another way of looking
at this tremendous guilt that I carry. It has
often seemed overwhelming. In a way I've
been getting an answer. I'm learning to
forgive myself, one piece at a time. I'm not
sure how it is happening, but it is. I feel
like my grief has given me different eyes.
I'm learning how to love myself and take
care of myself. Every once in a while I
have a glimpse of a compassionate, loving
person. I'm surprised when I see it is me.
This is one area of my grief that transcends

any therapy. I am learning to look at my loss and find meaning. This is indeed my miracle.

Sudden Death

According to the grief experts, sudden death, especially involving a child, is one of the most difficult deaths to grieve. Sudden death gives no warning. No time for good-byes. No taking care of unfinished business. Sudden death is abrupt. It takes children, young adults, parents and beloved grandparents. Sudden death leaves its survivors stunned.

When a child dies, so do the expectations of the parents for that child. Their sense of history and family legacy is gone. It seems out of the natural order of things for a child to die before his parents. The loss of a child is compounded when it involves a sudden death.

Comparing the Severity of Grief

Comparing the severity of one case of grief to another is really business for the professional. Someone who has lost his pet dog of eighteen years will experience grief. Someone whose abusive husband finally dies will experience grief. Someone whose terminally ill parent dies will experience grief.

A sudden death creates a ripple effect that penetrates the lives of the bereaved as well as the non-bereaved. All the dimensions that one goes through during the grief process are magnified by a sudden death.

How often people have said to me, "I shouldn't complain in front of you, after all my loss is nothing compared to yours." It is very difficult to respond to people who say that. Because I lost all my children doesn't diminish the singular loss another person experiences. To suggest that I have a "corner on the market" of grief is indeed intimidating.

I tell people who ask how I survived my terrible tragedy about my positioning theory. In the marketing world businesses "position" a product in the minds of the consumer. It is most difficult to re-position or give a new look to an old product and maintain the product recognition. So too with grief. Like a new product, each "death" has to be positioned. Grief is a process of re-positioning one's loss over and over again.

Shortly after my children died a therapist friend gave me a book, *For Those I Love*, by a man named Martin Gray, a survivor of the holocaust who lost his entire family at Auschwitz. Gray went on to marry and have five beautiful daughters. One tragic day in France he drove up the mountain to his chateau and found the house on fire. All his children and wife perished.

His story helped me position myself with regard to my own loss. Ten being the worst, I gave myself a six. I was somehow comforted in knowing that there were others who had so much more loss to deal with than I did. Not really feeling proud of this strange comfort, I share it with you anyway.

Marvin Gray went on to set up a foundation to help people cope with loss. He carved a meaning out of his incredible life tragedies. His story gave me strength. His story helped me to feel for others in the depths of my own sorrow. His story kept flashing through my mind. There is hope. No matter how great or small our loss.

The death of my own children was far more difficult for me than the death of my brother while I was a teenager. When my brother died he had had so much pain from his cancer that his death was in a sense, welcomed. He suffered for two years. He was five-feet, eight inches tall and weighed sixty-five pounds when he died. It was the end of a tremendous amount of suffering for him. It was the end of a long battle for my parents.

Before my children died, they were healthy and vibrant. It wasn't real. It was real. One day they were riding their bikes, playing music, eating popcorn. Eight hours later they were all dead.

Society and Grief

Why do many grief professionals consider it important to the grief process to view the deceased?

Viewing the deceased is critical in coming to terms with the reality of the loss. Omitting it often causes prolonged denial and triggers other grief reactions.

However, many people feel very uncomfortable when faced with the business of viewing a deceased friend or family member. Some people are shocked or frightened by the sight of a dead body. Understanding that it is *normal* to look different when you are dead is half the battle. For some reason (maybe denial) we seem to be shocked when a friend doesn't look the same as when we last saw her. But she's *supposed* to look different. Her entire body has stopped.

Viewing the dead is healthy. There is nothing morbid about it. Just because we might feel squeamish or afraid (maybe of our own mortality) does not mean that we should eliminate this process.

People often will say that when they die, they don't want anybody looking at their body. One cannot help but think that these people are not thinking of their loved ones, but only of themselves.

The Importance of Viewing the Deceased

Funerals, wakes, and memorial services are part of the theological and secular traditions of our grieving rituals.[8] The theological part is our way of honoring our deceased loved one. The secular parts of these traditions are for the living, not the dead. When we have allowed our vanity and ego to follow us to the grave, countless mourners get short-changed in their grief process.

A guest lecturer for a hospice spoke about her seventeen-year-old daughter's death in a car accident. The mother decided that she wanted the casket open. She knew, even though it would be difficult for some, the importance of allowing her daughter's friends the final good-bye. She had the funeral director put two signs at the entrance hallway to the funeral home. "Go to the right if you would like to view your friend, or to the left, if you would like to memorialize her via a graduation picture." She said that 95 percent of the people went to the right for a final good-bye.

In many discussions about viewing the body, people say that they want to remember their friend or family member "the way she was." But grief experts say that just isn't a good idea; it does not cement the reality of the loss. Many say the grief process takes much longer when the deceased is not viewed.

ॐ

I feel strongly that the grief experts are right, because I chose not to view my children. I don't know why. Maybe it was fear. I regret that decision. I will regret it for the rest of my life. My grief frequently reverts back to such questions as: What were they wearing; what did they look like; were they burned; did someone fix their hair ...? I wish that the funeral director or a close friend had intervened and strongly encouraged my ex-husband and me to view the children. But no one did. I never saw my children after they died. I know what the experts are talking about when they say viewing is important as part of the grief process. I know what it has been like because I didn't.

During the trial over the cause of the fire involving the death of my children, an envelope was delivered to my attorneys in court. I was sitting at the table nearest the messenger, so I put out my hand to receive the envelope and was told it wasn't anything I'd really want to see. The envelope was then snatched out of my hands. It didn't take me long to find out that the envelope contained pictures of the children after they were found by the fire department. I did not look at those pictures until a year later.

When my brother died I was listening to his heart with a stethoscope. He had been in a coma for four days. It was around 9 p.m. on a Thursday. As I was listening to his heart, it started to beat real fast. And then nothing. I listened again. Nothing. The nurse came in. My brother was dead. But to me there was no difference. He looked the same as he had just a few minutes before. He just stopped breathing. In a way his death was very simple. His spirit just slipped quietly away. It was the only time I ever saw a human being die.

Next door to my brother was a little four-year-old girl named Dolly who had a rare heart disease. Her parents very seldom came to see her because they were afraid they might be present when she died. As fate would have it, Dolly's parents were next door the night my brother died. My parents invited them in to say a prayer before my brother's body was taken away. Dolly's parents visited her every day after my brother died. She died two weeks after my brother.

At the funeral home I saw my brother in the casket. He was dressed in his pajamas. I was there when they closed the casket. I said good-bye to John – finally at peace.

How I wish I had that memory of my children.

What behavioral changes should we expect from the bereaved?

People who are recently bereaved often become "difficult" as far as friendships go. A previously friendly, concerned, giving, understanding, considerate friend might seem to change character when struck by a tragedy. A few of the behavior changes are loss of memory, irritability, fatigue, repetition, disorganization, withdrawal, and a yearning for the deceased. A recently bereaved friend is not an easy friend to have. A bereaved friend might not respond to your letters, might decline social invitations, might not ask for help or simply indicate she is doing "fine." The bereaved send out a lot of mixed messages. As you can see, it is most difficult to read what your friend is really needing. If you are consistent and predictable in your support, it will allow your bereaved friend to focus on what she can depend upon.

The Bereaved Send Out a Lot of Mixed Messages

So if your bereaved friend is acting weird and unlike the "old" pal you thought you knew, be patient. Be there. Be persistent. Be consistent. Your friend is trying out behavior that will help her accept her loss. It's all trial and error. She will get better. Give her time.

❧

Because I left my home community shortly after the fire to live in Chicago, I cut myself off from the town that I had grown to love and work in. Over time I stopped hearing from all but a few people. I cannot tell you how often I looked for notes from someone just telling me they were thinking of me. I used to play a game with myself. I would check the mail every fourth day to increase my chances of receiving mail. I still feel "good" when my mailbox is full.

There was a long period of time where I could not write. My attention span was zero. I couldn't read. I'd forget phone numbers or addresses. One particular time, shortly after the fire, I found myself coming out of an appointment and went totally blank as to where I was, where my office was; I temporarily forgot all phone numbers. From then on I always had addresses and phone numbers available on my person.

I didn't know how to tell my friends about these odd things that were happening to me. Some figured I didn't want to hear from them because I didn't respond to their notes. It was a vicious circle of disorganized events I didn't understand. How did I expect my friends to understand?

I still find comfort in old friends from years ago who have come into my life again. Some never even knew the children. I have friends new and old that have persisted, week after week, month after month, year after year, supporting me, never hurrying me, never judging me and most of all encouraging me to keep on going. My friends were my eyes for a long time. They saw the future for me when I saw none.

I know there are some permanent changes in my personality and behavior since my children's deaths. I know that much of the "old" Johnette will never return. I am beginning to like the "new" me and so are my friends. They accept me changes and all.

Most of my friends have never lost a child. My loss has changed their lives in many ways. We have all grown together. None of our lives will ever be the same.

Is there such thing as societal grief?

A well-publicized event like the Challenger disaster triggers grief reactions in many people and often stirs up old or hidden grief. Sometimes all it takes is a sad movie or news clip to awaken that part of us that we don't really know too much about. Societal grief catches us.

Such media events shock us; we feel our own terror and fear caused from our own grief (although we don't recognize it as such). For some reason (probably denial) we think IT can never happen to us. Our tears are often a release of that fear.

Whether it's seeing the stark reality of the famine in Somalia or the frozen dead body of a street person in Chicago, we feel for these strangers. Something in our gut hurts. Even though our losses might not be so big or so tragic, we identify with these people. We share in their grief because we've known it in our own lives, in our own way.

When my children died, the entire community mourned their deaths. Many parents told me stories of their kids being afraid to sleep in a darkened room or refusing to close their bedroom doors. Some friends stopped using wood to heat their houses. Others took long overdue vacations. One friend took a two-month summer sabbatical from her job to be with her kids for the first time in twelve years. One couple started marriage counseling trying to preserve what they had been ready to toss out. My daughter's teacher left her teaching job that summer to relocate to a new community. One friend told me the sound of fire trucks still reminds her and her family of the fire. One mother told me that there isn't a day that goes by that she doesn't think of me and the kids as she sends her teenagers off to school each morning, wondering if she will ever see them again.

I can remember when I was first married, asking a friend who taught theology and philosophy why, with all the tragedy in the world, was I able to be relatively happy. He told me that tragedies come in many disguises. For some it could be loneliness; for others, old age; for some, homelessness; and for still others, death. It doesn't have to be big and grand to qualify. As I'm writing this, I realize he never answered my question.

Is it important to discuss the circumstance surrounding a death with the bereaved?

Openly going over the events surrounding a death is invaluable to the bereaved, whether adult or child. They need to ask questions and listen to the answers in order to begin to process their loss.

Repeating the Circumstances of the Death Helps the Bereaved

It is not at all unusual in sudden deaths (murders, suicides, etc.) for survivors to go back to the "scene of a crime," sometimes five or ten years after the fact, to resolve nagging, unanswered questions surrounding the death. This process can be tedious and repetitious to a non-bereaved friend. But it is critical to the overall grief work. Be patient. Listen. Listen. And listen.

The lawsuit over the cause of the house fire involving the deaths of my children allowed me to speak with different experts about the fire. I had many practical – as well as morbid-sounding – questions. I talked about the fire and its causes for two years. Always looking for new information or a hidden meaning in information I already had. I still appreciate someone sharing with me her story of that night. Contrary to what people sometimes believe, I want to hear about it. I always will.

Is there a proper or improper way to grieve?

How one person grieves depends on an infinite number of variables, unique to each person. Culture, religion, education, age and gender all come into play when we grieve.

However some general guidelines may be helpful when a person experiences grief. Not all people will go through all the stages or dimensions of grief. But for sure, grief affects everyone.

If the response to grief gradually moves a person into resolution and acceptance of his loss, then he is probably working through his grief. If his response to grief creates abnormal life changes, then he probably hasn't resolved his grief issues.

We are beginning to see that the business of grief is important. How non-bereaved people respond to a given grief situation can make a big difference to the person who has lost a loved one. Being aware and informed about the grief process helps everyone communicate more clearly when faced with a loss.

I think of one of my children more often than another. Usually it is my daughter. I then feel guilty. I find it impossible to grieve the children as a group, although I try. I still get the guilts when I think about just one of them. I feel that I should think of them all equally. I try to "grieve the group," but it doesn't work.

I think it is natural for the bereaved to have many different feelings about what is "proper" grieving and what it isn't. Some people will not party, go to movies, go out to eat, dance, wear vibrant colors, socialize or eat certain foods for a specific amount of time – or ever in some cases. All of this is okay. Because one person sets his own boundaries in terms of his mourning doesn't mean another person will set the same boundaries.

Why is it appropriate to mention the name of the deceased to the bereaved?

It is extremely important to mention the name of the deceased so the bereaved can work through their grief into resolution and acceptance of their loss.

Many times we feel uncomfortable bringing up the memory of the deceased. We often wonder if we are going to trigger a sad reaction or upset the bereaved. Mentioning the name of the deceased makes it clear to our bereaved friend that their loved one is not forgotten and that his existence did make a difference. It is important for the bereaved to know that others miss and remember their loved one.

I don't think there is a more comforting gesture than a friend fondly sharing a brief story about one of my children. I am always touched when someone else remembers the children. I like to hear their names spoken out loud.

One friend whose son had died in a car accident said her daughter had recently mentioned to her how much she missed her brother. She wondered why they never

used his name in conversation around the
house anymore.

My friend said she really hadn't realized
they were all sort of tip-toeing around his
death. His memory was very much alive in
his mother's heart. They all decided to
take a few minutes each week and tell
funny stories about their brother and son.

Does having faith help cure grief?

It was suggested to me that this is a very
personal question and really shouldn't be
asked. I disagree.

Faith in a kind and loving God often
provides comfort for the recently
bereaved. Faith transcends any human
dimensions we have so far talked about
when dealing with grief. The theology of
an afterlife, of the spirit continuing on into
another level of being, can help the
bereaved accept their loss.

The death of a loved one challenges
many of our steadfast beliefs, not the least
of which is religion. To profess a faith is
one thing. To actually apply a theological
dogma when challenged with the death of
a loved one is another. Death has a way of
cracking many long-held beliefs and
traditions. Death forces us to look at the
attic of our souls. Often we find theologies
that still have price tags. New, but never

It's Not Unusual to Blame God for the Loss of a Loved One

worn. Sometimes these theologies, when called upon, don't fit.

It is not uncommon at all for a "fairly religious," newly bereaved person to blame God for his loss. If our perception of God is of someone sitting at a computer screen deciding whom He will persecute, kill, starve, mutilate, or make suffer, then we need to change the terminology from God to monster. Belief that God allows certain tragic events to occur to "teach us lessons" or "test our faith" is for many a difficult theology. Who among us can honestly say we can love and trust a God who works from such a vantage point?

When we combine the reality of death with the workings of our individual human souls, we will come up with many different combinations: for some of us, a formalized religion, for others a life-long personal philosophy, and for still others no particular belief in anything but themselves.

As I approached my thirties I had weeded out what parts of my Catholic upbringing worked for me and what did not. I was not a rigid, traditional Catholic. I practiced birth control and was contemplating divorce.

The morning of the fire a local clergyman came to talk to me. He sat next to me on my mother's couch and told me it was God's will that my children and housekeeper died in this tragic fire. I gently told this clergyman that I appreciated his concern but that I did not believe in the God he was talking about. I did not believe in a God that took four young lives so tragically. My God was loving and kind. He was not destructive or vindictive. He had nothing to do with the fire. I knew that. But that was about all I knew.

I stood at the cemetery and looked at the three white caskets containing my children. I was struck by the crazy irony of it all. I had spent the last eleven years mothering and taking care of their every need. And here I was burying them on a cold March day. Leaving them in this place called a cemetery. My cherubs, as I so frequently called them. I was numbed. But I knew there was something that I didn't understand. Their lives could not have been for nothing. Their spirits could not have died.

Through my grief process I have studied many religious beliefs. I joke that I finally came up with around one hundred fifty-six reasons why the fire happened. Some religious, and some not. Slowly, one by one, they didn't work anymore. Instead of reasons I began to find causes. Causes that needed me and my experiences.

I have found that much of my "faith" was in other people. My children, my husband, my work, my community. When all of this was taken away, I found little faith left inside. What had happened to all the great theologies that I had stored up for a rainy day?

My grief process has opened up the spiritual quadrant of my life, which Elisabeth Kübler-Ross talks about in her Life Death Transition seminars. I had never really even thought about that part of me. I guess I had taken that all for granted. I didn't call on my heart very often for answers. I always looked externally, out in the world. The spiritual part was all new to me. Trust myself? Ask myself for answers? Look within? Question my long-held traditions? Admit that something was very wrong? Realize that most of my intellectual conclusions about life and death were just that, intellectual. And when tested, just didn't work.

I attended Kübler-Ross' Life Death Transition workshop three years after the children's deaths. It was a turning point in my grief process. I felt loved. It was different. It flashed bits of forgiveness at me. I wanted more. I didn't know how I was going to make the inner journey I knew I had to make. But I knew it had begun.

I wouldn't call myself religious, but I have faith. I know that my children are physically dead but spiritually alive. I know in order to continue on in this life, I need to learn forgiveness of myself and others. Whatever else I do with my life will be a direct result of that forgiveness. I have learned the God in my life comes to me through people – not churches, or rituals, or rules, or theologies, but people. I feel I am emerging from my grief with a renewed faith in life and its natural transition, death. I'm afraid of neither.

Families and Grief

Can children grieve?

Children go through the same grief processes that adults do, but with one major difference: Children grieve according to the developmental and cognitive stage they are in at the time of their loss. For example, a three-year-old will show his grief intermittently. His inability to use words and express himself often tricks adults into thinking that he is unaffected. But he is very much affected. Children in this age group express their bewilderment over the separation that has occurred in their lives in anxious behavior, regression, or in developing attachments to familiar objects around them.

Children mourn as early as six months. But the common thread that they carry through to their young adulthood is their undeveloped coping capacity and resulting vulnerability. Whether it is a teenager who doesn't want to show his feelings because he doesn't want to be different or an infant who shows distress but doesn't really know why, grief touches their young lives. It is up to us, as adults, to educate ourselves about our own grief so we will understand and be able to help our children. Children have a much bigger challenge when dealing with grief than we do because of their developmental and cognitive limitations.

I remember the story that Dr. Sandra Fox told at a hospice lecture in Hanover, New Hampshire. A young boy of eight lost his grandmother to a long-term illness. The family had shared much of the illness so the death was expected. When it came time to go to the wake, the young boy refused to go see his grandmother. No one understood. He loved his grandmother so much. They brought in a friend to talk with him. How perceptive they were. The boy told the family friend that there was no way he was going to see his grandmother with her head cut off. The friend asked incredulously what he meant. He said the night before he had heard his father and mother talking about how his grandmother "had lost her head."

As an eleven-year-old I lost my best friend to leukemia. I remember going to see her every day after school. She always loved that. My parents told me Virginia was sick. I really did not understand what they meant, but I knew something was very wrong. When she died my parents told me she had died on the way to the hospital. I kept having visions of her struggling in the back seat of this big black car. At eleven years old I didn't really understand how someone died.

When I was at my children's wake a friend of my daughter's (age nine) came to me crying. He told me he had always wanted to marry Johnette and now he didn't know what he was going to do. I shared with him the story of my best friend and how I had felt the same way when she died. I didn't know how life was going to feel without her around any more. I told him that it did get better and that I had never forgotten my friend. And that he would never forget his friend, my daughter, either. I told him that feeling sad was okay. He's the only person I remember speaking with at the wake.

What is unique for a parent about the loss of an adult child?

We often think that the older someone is, the more experience they have in dealing with death. When an adult child dies, usually his spouse or children make all the funeral arrangements. The parent is often left in the background, sometimes for practical reasons: The parents might live in another state or be elderly. The family might conclude that they are sparing them the unnecessary burden of arranging the funeral. By the time the parents fly in, the arrangements are often made. The parents might not even have had a chance to say good-bye to their adult child if the body was sent directly to a crematory.

When we think about it, especially from a mother's point of view, we are there when our children are born, we certainly want to be there when they die. The grief process doesn't have preference about age. It touches everyone. Parents don't grieve less because they are older or because their child was an adult. As sad as it is when parents survive their child, they want to be there when the child dies. It seems normal and logical that the parent of an adult child would be treated as a primary survivor, but that is not the way it usually happens.

Parents of adult children have multiple problems to deal with. Many times they have retired to a new area in the country and have made new friends. When they arrive back home, their world is untouched by their tragedy. They might not have many living friends to act as a support group. They might not be physically well, and now have the added problem of dealing with the emotional suffering over their loss.

If Their Adult Child Dies, Parents May See Less and Less of Beloved Grandchildren

Parents of adult children may have been financially dependent on their child. The child's death may mean an end to that support. Parents will see less and less of their grandchildren if the surviving spouse remarries. There may be ambivalence on the part of the parents over the death of their adult child if it was due to alcoholism, complications of AIDS, suicide, or other "taboo" illnesses. It is true that parents have more memories to recall, so their grief often takes longer.

Remember to ask your friends who have buried an adult child how they are doing. We frequently ask how the grandchildren and surviving spouse are doing and forget the parents. Remember they are grieving also!

The AIDS epidemic has added an extra dimension to this problem. AIDS is taking away the lives of hundreds of thousands of young people, so many parents are experiencing the deaths of their adult children. Unlike parents of cancer victims, who are often inundated with offers of help, many parents of AIDS victims are outcast from their social network.

Many times it is the mother who ends up living with her adult child as primary support, with the father unable to accept his adult child's fate.

Unlike the parents we talked about above, these parents are faced with dealing with their own shame and righteousness over their adult child's illness. Their own prejudices and feelings of guilt are not easily shared with anyone. Their long-time friends and supports disappear, often out of fear and ignorance. Bank accounts dry up. These parents are faced with the enormous responsibility of finding affordable care and emotional strength to support their adult child. The suffering they see is incomprehensible.

AIDS can attack the body with one illness after another, each worse than the other. Parents of these adults or children sit hopelessly by, watching their child slowly die a cruel, relentless death, in surroundings that are often inadequate and degrading. They are often alone.

Parents who meet the challenge of unconditionally supporting their adult child dying of the many complications of

AIDS need our recognition and help. They need informed and understanding support people who are non-judgmental and loving. If there ever was a time we need to effectively support the bereaved it is now.

What are the unique elements in the grief over the loss of a grandchild?

Grandparents are blessed for being exactly that, grandparents. They have reached a point in their lives where they begin to see the fruits of their life's labors. Their children are independent and committed to their own lives and families; they see their grandchildren as "chips off the old block." A sense of pride and accomplishment surrounds their lives; they see themselves being a part of the future in their grandchildren. Grandparenting can be a time to fulfill long-awaited dreams. And then they lose a grandchild.

The grief process isn't any different for a grandparent than for anyone else, except their grief is doubled. Not only do they grieve for the loss of their grandchild, which must seem totally out of sync with the order of things, but they grieve for their own child and the pain she is going through; they often feel helpless and inadequate.

֍

My children were blessed with grandparents right next door. My parents. And they had their paternal grandmother less than two hours away. We moved back to Vermont so that they would have a quality to their lives that was not available to them in suburban Washington, D.C. That was probably one of the most important decisions my ex-husband and I ever made as a couple.

The children would call Gram next door and ask her what was for dinner almost daily. They loved my parents and each child had a special relationship with them. Their paternal grandmother treated them like royalty. Their visits to her house could not be missed.

My parents' only son died of cancer at the age of twelve. The death of their three grandchildren would seem to be the final straw. But somehow, probably because of their strong faith and relationship with one another, they weathered this holocaust.

My mother loved my children as if they were her own. And they loved her deeply. We are all lucky to have had that love, even if it was for such a short time.

What effect does the death of a child have on a marriage?

Studies suggest that more than seventy percent of married couples who lose a child end up divorced. (This figure increases to more than ninety percent when that loss involves a murder.) This astounding statistic suggests that something is drastically wrong with the dynamics of couple-grieving.

The grief process is unique to each individual, so when grief touches a couple, it becomes compounded. No two people are going to grieve in the same way, at the same time, or with the same intensity. The guilt, the denial, the anger, the bargaining will be different and come at different times for each person. Many couples blame each other and get stuck in their grief process. One may move on while another stays put.

As we learn to understand and respect the grief process, we will begin to acknowledge the difficult challenge that two people have when faced with a shared or common loss.

The Compassionate Friends is a self-help group of bereaved parents organized to help couples and single parents whose children have died. This organization has been very successful in bringing parents together to share in their common grief. Many more organizations are springing up across the country.

Because I had been separated from my husband for six months at the time of the fire, I no longer shared much with him. We attempted to get together and sort out pictures and a few personal effects of the children shortly after the fire. We usually ended up crying and asking why.

It was a very difficult time for me. I was scared and very much alone. Three days after the funeral I went to a local bank and borrowed money to live on. I did not know how I would repay it at the time. A cousin flew in from Chicago to be with me and help me deal with the business of the fire. I don't know what I would have done without him.

An inventory needed to be done on the house for insurance purposes. My husband said he could not do it with me. I went through every room in that house with my sister and two close friends. We worked for a few days and then quit. A few days later we'd start at it again. The house was built in 1856 and had thirteen rooms.

I remember the day I gave a seventy-five-page inventory of the house to my husband. That same day I put my parents on a plane to Europe. By that evening I had checked into our local hospital. I stayed there for ten days. I was emotionally and physically exhausted.

I did not return to Vermont for a whole year. When I did it was to settle my divorce. I had not seen my husband or really talked to him in a year. The divorce was sad. It was final. I felt responsible. I remember flying back to Chicago not caring about anything. I think it was the only time in my grief process that I really consciously thought about suicide. I didn't care if the plane landed or not. There was nothing left in my life. I blamed myself for everything. Even my divorce.

After I returned to Vermont two years later my ex-husband and I met for lunch a few times a year. We shared memories about our children. It is always comforting to see him. He reminds me so much of my sons.

I have seen many couples grieving together. Often, one will want to talk about their deceased child, while the other will not. Seldom does a grieving couple feel like a movie or getting out at the same time. Partying is considered taboo by one and a release by another.

Having fun again is a difficult passage to go through in the grief cycle. Having done it alone I can't imagine having to do it with one eye always on another person wondering how he's feeling. I was so absorbed in my own grief I don't know if I could have found room for someone else's. No wonder many couples don't make it.

Do men grieve differently than women?

Males have traditionally been brought up to believe that outward expressions of feelings (sadness, loneliness, loss) are not masculine and suggest weakness of character. Such "macho" characteristics put men in direct conflict with the grief process. They are not open to the "feeling" process that is critical to grief work. That doesn't mean that men don't experience the feelings. They usually just don't know how to express them, or feel uncomfortable doing so.

Traditionally, women have had a much easier time with expressing feelings. The anger and control aspects of grief have been difficult for some women to come to grips with, whereas men seem to be able to express themselves better with those emotions.

We've assigned feminine and masculine characteristics to the grief process, when in fact grief has no gender. Women are

supposed to grieve this way, and men are
supposed to be strong. This stereotyping
doesn't work.

Males have a tough challenge when
faced with grief either from a bereaved or
non-bereaved point of view.

A friend of mine found out he had AIDS.
He was forty-two and had two beautiful
grown daughters. He caught AIDS from a
first-time male lover. When he was
diagnosed, his family (Irish Catholic; he
was one of seven boys) disowned him.
His daughters kept their distance. His wife
filed for divorce.

I shared with my friend how I wish I
could have traded places with him. He
was seriously thinking of ending his hell,
and I was trying to find a reason to live in
mine. Our lives were different but alike.
Playwrights. He needed to write an
ending, I needed to start a whole new
play. We didn't come to any earth-
shattering conclusions, other than we
decided that we needed to find meaning
in our present lives in order to get by,
even for just a day.

He went on to lecture to hospice
organizations, etc. His ability to share his
life experience even up to his death
touched innumerable lives, including
mine. We transcended my femininity and
his masculinity. We were one in our grief.

Footnotes

1 – (page 10): *On Death and Dying;* Kübler-Ross, E.; 1969.
2 – (pages 19): *Death Etiquette for the 90s: What to Do/ What to Say;* Hartnett, J; 1993.
3 – (page 24) :*Grief counseling and Grief Therapy;* Worden, J.W.; 1982.
4 – (page 25): *Loss and Anticipatory Grief;* Rando, T.A., 1986.
5 – (pages 33, 71): *Children and Grief: Big Issues for Little Hearts;* Hartnett, J; 1993.
6 – (page 38): *Grief in the Workplace: 40 Hours Plus Overtime;* Hartnett, J; 1993.
7 – (page 48): *Different Losses Different Issues: What to Expect and How to Help;* Hartnett, J; 1993.
8 – (page 57): *The Funeral: An Endangered Tradition ~ Making Sense of the Final Farewell;* Hartnett, J; 1993.

References

Aries, P., (1981). The hour of our death. New York: Oxford University Press.

DeSpelder, L.A., & Strickland, A.L. (1987). The last dance. 2nd ed. California: Mansfield Publishing Co.

Freud, S. (1955). Mourning and meloncholia. In J. Rickman, M.D. (Ed.), A general selection from the works of Sigmund Freud. New York: Doubleday.

Kastenbaum, R.J. (1991). Death, society, and human experience.New York: Merrill/Macmillan Publishing Co.

Kübler-Ross, E. (1975). Death the final stage of growth. Prentice-Hall: New Jersey.

Kübler-Ross, E. (1981). Living with death and dying. New York: Macmillan Publishing Co.

Kübler-Ross, E. (1969). On death and dying. New York: Macmillan Publishing Co.

Rando, T.A. (1984). Grief, dying and death. Illinois: Research Press.

Rando, T.A. (1986). Loss and anticipatory grief. Massachusetts/ Toronto: Lexington Books.

Rando, T.A. (1986). Parental loss of a child. Illinois: Research Press.

Schneider, J. (1984). Stress, loss, and grief. Maryland; Aspen Publication.

Stephenson, J.S. (1985). Death, grief, and mourning. New York: The Free Press.Wolfelt, A.D. (1988). Death and grief a guide for clergy. Indiana: Accelerated Development Inc.

Wass, H., Berardo, F.M., Neimeyer, R.A., (1988). Dying: facing the facts; 2nd ed.; Washington: Hemisphere Publishing Corp.

Worden, J.W. (1982). Grief counseling and grief therapy. New York: Springer Publishing Co.

Prepare yourself for one of the most difficult jobs you'll ever have: Grief.

If your bookstore or employer does not have the other books in this series, please indicate which ones and how many you need on the form below; cost of each book is $6.95, or $29.95 for the set.

Good Mourning also publishes a set of sympathy note cards (and envelopes) with artwork designed by children who have died. Included is a bookmark with suggested messages of sympathy, to facilitate your own written expression of sympathy to the bereaved – a poignant and personal way to express your sympathy. The cost of a set of 12 note cards/bookmarks is $9.95, plus postage and handling. Please send a check or money order for the total to:

**Good Mourning
P.O. 9355
South Burlington, VT 05407-9355**

Name of Book	Quantity	Each	Price
Using Grief to Grow: A Primer *How You Can Help/How to Get Help*		$6.95	
Different Losses Different Issues: *What to Expect and How to Help.*		$6.95	
The Funeral: An Endangered Tradition *Making Sense of the Final Farewell*		$6.95	
Grief in the Workplace: *40 Hours Plus Overtime*		$6.95	
Children and Grief: *Big Issues for Little Hearts*		$6.95	
Death Etiquette for the '90s: *What to Do/ What to Say*		$6.95	
Set of Six Books		$29.95	
Note Cards (one dozen, plus envelopes)		$9.95	
Subtotal			
Tax, if applicable			
Shipping/handling ($2.25 ea/$8 set)			
Total (check enclosed)			

Phone: 802-658-5883

Ship to:

*Name*_____

*Address*_____

*City*_____*State*_____*ZIP*_____

If you would like to submit a question regarding the death of a loved one, or learn how to support a friend who has lost a loved one, please do so in the space below or on your paper. I will be happy to respond to as many questions as I can.

With warmest regards, Johnette Hartnett

_____

_____

_____

_____

_____

_____

_____

_____

_____

_____

_____

_____

_____

_____

_____

_____

_____

_____

_____